A TASTE OF EMPIRE

A TASTE
OF EMPIRE

Imperial Cuisine™ with Chef Maximo Cortés
A Demonstration

JOVANNI SY

Talonbooks

Talonbooks
278 East First Avenue, Vancouver, British Columbia, Canada V5T 1A6
talonbooks.com

First printing: 2017

Typeset in Scala
Printed and bound in Canada on 100% post-consumer recycled paper

Cover design by Typesmith
Interior design by Chloë Filson

Rights to produce *A Taste of Empire*, in whole or in part, in any medium by
any group, amateur or professional, are retained by the author. Interested
persons are requested to contact Talonbooks at 278 East First Avenue,
Vancouver, British Columbia, Canada V5T 1A6; telephone (toll-free)
888-445-4176; email: info@talonbooks.com; talonbooks.com.

Talonbooks acknowledges the financial support of the Canada Council for
the Arts, the Government of Canada through the Canada Book Fund, and
the Province of British Columbia through the British Columbia Arts Council
and the Book Publishing Tax Credit.

Library and Archives Canada Cataloguing in Publication

Sy, Jovanni, author
        A taste of empire / Jovanni Sy.

A play.
Foreword by Guillermo Verdecchia.
ISBN 978-1-77201-160-9 (softcover)

        I. Verdecchia, Guillermo, writer of foreword II. Title.

PS8637.Y2T37 2017   C812'.6   C2017-900730-0

*To GLV – collaborator, friend, and inspiration
to a generation of artists*

*There is no document of civilization which is not
at the same time a document of barbarism.*
> —Walter Benjamin,
> "Theses on the Philosophy of
> History, VII" in *Illuminations*
> (trans. Harry Zohn, 1969)

Contents

Foreword

Grub first, ethics later.   —Bertolt Brecht

When I give food to the poor, they call me a saint.
When I ask why the poor have no food, they call
me a communist.   —Hélder Câmara

good capture the spirit of America?

Tell me what you eat, and I will tell you who
you are.   —Brillat-Savarin

"Food," someone on the CBC said recently, "is the zeitgeist of the decade." Certainly, in North America, we can't turn around these days without bumping up against something related to food. My entirely unscientific research shows currently more than 86,000 TV programs are dedicated to food: food as spectacle, food as lifestyle, food as destination, food as agon, food as representation of the psychic lives of chefs. A quick Google search turns up 37.8 million food books: food as memoir and/or nostalgia, studies of food in literature, disquisitions on food to make you well, to make you more spiritual or authentic, food *manifesti*, and, yes, cookbooks. The Internet overflows with food. It's stuffed with food-based memes: diet-related ones; racist ones about ethnic food; as well, of course, as cats and dogs looking funny or cute or sad or happy in relation to food. And then there are those Instagram things of meals not yet eaten that people feel compelled to post. While I'm not sure the CBC correspondent used the word "zeitgeist" with absolute precision, there is no question she had accurately identified *something*. Food has a new cultural status here. If food isn't exactly the zeitgeist, it is a new and powerful (floating) signifier able to absorb all sort of meanings. It is, perhaps, a whole new medium.

I'm not anti-food. (I just put a pinch of truffle salt in my mashed potatoes.) I grow food in my garden. I'm especially proud of my wild arugula, my San Marzano tomatoes, and my peppers: jalapeños, serranos, the Habaneros (red, orange, and white), and, most of all, the Naga Vipers. I like food – as does Jovanni Sy, who concocted *A Taste of Empire*. In fact, Jovanni secured my assistance for the show when he suggested that the first thing we should do to develop the piece was get together in a kitchen to cook, talk, and eat. We sipped a crisp white wine and snacked on manchego and crackers while he chopped and stirred. I thought, "This is my sort of rehearsal. I definitely want to work on this piece if Jovanni's going to be cooking and feeding me." And feed me he did. I've eaten enough rehearsal bangus to claim I too used to be Filipino.

Like I said: I like food. What troubles me (and many others), and what Jovanni addresses in *A Taste of Empire*, is the way food, in much contemporary North American culture, has been gutted of its history and abstracted from socio-economic realities. Which makes sense, really. A floating signifier wouldn't float if it wasn't empty.

Using the apparently simple structure of preparing a meal – dramaturgically simple, though practically speaking it's a ridiculously complex undertaking (let me take this moment to thank our amazing stage managers and sous-sous-chefs) – Jovanni has created a performance that reveals the many economic and ethical entanglements to which contemporary globalization has given rise. *A Taste of Empire* takes the now familiar public performance of food preparation, and, using a classic comic *naïf*, messes up the slick demonstration we have come to expect. Food – actual food – is messy; food prep is messy; and food's historical, cultural, geographic, and political entanglements are messier still. *A Taste of Empire* asks: What does globalization taste like?

Brecht, who (like his character Galileo) had nothing against a good meal and was sensitive to the ethics of eating, disliked what he called culinary theatre, by which he meant theatre that was easily digested, theatre that satisfied its audience's simplest appetites, but left them fundamentally unnourished. Jovanni has taken the notion of culinary theatre and turned it on its head. He said he got the idea for the show while watching a sushi chef work one night – and thinking that the chef's dexterous performance was more engaging than many plays he'd seen recently. He sensed an opportunity to do something special in the preparation and sharing of a meal with an audience. Like other productions and performances that have centred around the preparation of food – Robin Soans's *The Arab-Israeli Cookbook*, Fast Forward's *Feeding Frenzy*, Seven Fingers' *Cuisine and Confessions*, not to mention the Futurist and Surrealist banquets – neither Jovanni nor I make any claim to be the first to have done this – an important part of the performance is the sense of conviviality the preparation and sharing of food engenders. (You want an audience to hang out after a show and chat? Give them something to eat.) Unlike many of those other food-inspired shows, however, *A Taste of Empire* poses a challenge to its audience: now that you know something of the histories that inform this meal, the *stuff* this meal is made of ... do you still want to eat it? I suspect Brecht would have savoured that contradiction, even while enjoying the tasty rellenong bangus Jovanni prepared.

I trust you will too.

—Guillermo "Chimichurri" Verdecchia

Production History

A *Taste of Empire* was first presented by Cahoots Theatre
Company and performed at the Market Kitchen, a test kitchen
at the St. Lawrence Market in Toronto, June 30–July 24, 2010,
with the following cast and crew:

Written and performed by Jovanni Sy
Directed by Guillermo Verdecchia
Video design by David Yee
Dramaturgy by Ric Knowles
Stage managed by Joanna Barrotta
Production managed by Dale Yim
Assistant stage management by Neha Ross
Publicity by Erika Rueter
Graphic design by Christine Mangosing
Photography by Keith Barker

The play was remounted in the Courtyard at Granville Island
Public Market from May 22–25, 2014. A second revival took
place as part of Boca del Lupo's Micro Performance Series and
was performed in Vancouver at the Liu Institute for Global
Issues at the University of British Columbia, November 17 and
18; at UBC Farm, November 19 and 20; and at the opening
of The Fishbowl performance space on Granville Island,
November 26–28, 2015, with the following cast and crew:

Written and performed by Jovanni Sy
Assisted onstage by Natalie Tin Yin Gan (2014)
Assisted onstage by Pedro Chamale (2015)
Directed by Sherry J. Yoon
Technical direction by Carey Dodge
Video design by David Yee
Produced by Dani Fecko (2014)

The play was presented in Cantonese as 食盡天下 with English and Simplified Chinese surtitles as a Rice and Beans Theatre production at Gateway Theatre in Richmond, British Columbia, in association with the Gateway Theatre Pacific Festival, September 15–17, 2016, with the following cast and crew:·

Written and directed by Jovanni Sy
Translated and performed by Derek Chan
Assisted onstage by Pedro Chamale
Stage managed by Teresa Leung
Surtitles by Curtis Li
Technical direction by Carey Dodge
Produced by Pedro Chamale
Publicity by Davey Calderon
Lighting operated by Matthew Symons

Characters

JOVANNI   Sous-Chef to Master Chef Maximo Cortés
NEHA[1]   Sous-Sous-Chef to the Master

Setting

Full professional demonstration kitchen with working cooktop, refrigerator, and wash-up sink. A video screen is installed which sometimes shows live close-ups of the cooking and, at other times, provides illustrations to complement the spoken text.

Although the original production was in a very luxe, well-furnished professional demonstration kitchen, subsequent remounts have been in an outdoor plaza, a theatre lobby, and a yurt. This show can be performed anywhere as long as you're creative (and hygienic).

---

[1]   In this printed text, my sous-sous-chef is named after the wonderful Neha Ross who was my assistant in the 2010 premiere.

In subsequent revivals, the names of the assistants changed to the actual first names of the also wonderful Natalie Gan and Pedro Chamale.

And when the fabulous Derek Chan took over my role in his translation 食盡天下, the sous-chef became "小陳" or "Little Chan."

All of this is to say, if you're ever performing this play, use your own name. The whole conceit of the show is "I see you, you see me, and we're acknowledging the reality of this situation ... (except for the parts I blatantly fabricated)."

A Taste of Empire

Part 1

THE KING OF CHEFS

PROJECTION: [title card]
A TASTE OF EMPIRE with Chef Maximo Cortés

*After guests are seated, they are served an
amuse-bouche. Guests are alerted that the cooking
demonstration is about to begin when the sound of
heavy-metal power chords draws their attention to
the projection screen.*

*PROJECTION: [video sequence]
an extended video sequence as described below*

The show opens with an over-the-top Iron Chef*–style
video montage with many different shots of Chef
Maximo glowering menacingly like the highly
unpleasant* enfant terrible *of the culinary world
that he is.*

NARRATOR

You've seen him on television. You've bought his bestselling
cookbooks. Now in Toronto for a limited engagement ... it's
the Demon Chef,[2] the Madman of the Kitchen, the Grand
Master of Imperial Cuisine™ ... Chef Maximo Cortés!

---

2   This moniker is a shout-out to Alvin Leung, self-described Demon Chef and
     chef-proprietor of the Michelin Star–awarded restaurant Bo Innovation in
     Hong Kong's Wan Chai district. Chef Alvin was a pioneer in fusing molecular
     gastronomy techniques with traditional Chinese cookery. I've enjoyed a few
     memorable meals at Bo Innovation thanks to good friend (and Chef Alvin's
     cousin) Andrew Sun. Chef Alvin, of course, subsequently became famous as
     one of the judges on CTV's *Masterchef Canada*.

PROJECTION: *[still images]*
*Chef Maximo standing in front of each of his
restaurants*

Chef Maximo is the renowned chef-proprietor of not one,
not two, but *three* three-Michelin-star restaurants: *Imperius*
in Tokyo, *Il Duce* in Rome, and his flagship halal restaurant in
Kabul: *Warlord*.

A self-taught prodigy, Maximo Cortés scandalized the
culinary world with his signature style of cooking known as
Imperial Cuisine™.

Food and Wine named him Chef of the Decade. He was
inducted into the Culinary Hall of Fame. And Microsoft
recently released the bestselling video game, *Maximo Cortés:
Kitchen Gangsta*.

Now, Chef Maximo is offering a once-in-a-lifetime
opportunity to a handful of elite connoisseurs – a private
demonstration. Soon, you too will learn the previously
untold secrets of Imperial Cuisine™. So prepare for the
experience of your life.

And now ... please welcome the Chef of Kings, the King
of Chefs ... Maximo Cortés!

Video ends.

*they make it
sound very
fancy and
interesting*

*cuisine related
to imperialism
around the world
(food given to us
because of
imperialism)*

*its real
meaning*

[handwritten margin notes: Authoritarian, mighty, looking down]

Part 2

HIS MOST-DEVOTED DISCIPLE

PROJECTION: [still image]
Mao-like portrait of Chef Maximo

Sous-Chef JOVANNI enters wearing a chef's jacket,
with his commis cap in his hands.

JOVANNI

Hi ... hi there ... is this mic on? Can you hear me? Umm ...
I am *not* Chef Maximo Cortés. Obviously. You can all
see that.

So ... I've got some really exciting – but bad, bad news.
Chef Maximo just called from his Gulfstream jet and, apparently, he's been called away on a culinary emergency.

One of his many VIP regulars requested Chef Maximo
for a special mission. He wouldn't say who – Chef Maximo
treats his clients' privacy as sacred. But I do happen to know
that Bono can't get enough of his empanadas. But you didn't
hear that from me. *[handwritten: Jovanni info]*

Me. Right. So, my name is Jovanni and I'm Chef
Maximo's number-one sous-chef. I've been cooking with
the master from the age of ten – that's when he rescued
me from that Romanian orphanage.[3] I owe everything to
Chef Maximo; he taught me all I know. And now I get to
teach you.

---

3   I remember one performance where this got a far more boisterous reaction
     than usual. After the show when I was serving the bangus, some audience
     members starting speaking to me in Romanian. I had to explain twice that I
     wasn't actually Romanian, that it was just my attempt at ludicrous humour.
     I learned that sometimes when you say things in public, people are highly
     motivated to believe you ... all evidence to the contrary.

[handwritten: people easily influenced by people in power positions]

[handwritten: Theme? important?]

5

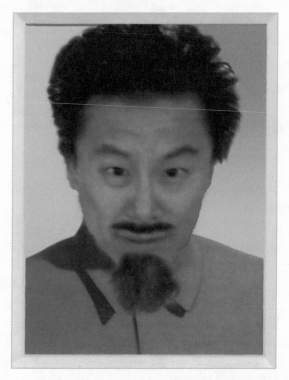

Chef Maximo in one of his more jovial moods

So, before we begin, Chef Maximo told me to pass on two messages to all of you. First, he regrets not being here but wants to assure you that I am qualified to give the exact same demonstration he would have given. Second, there are no refunds.

So let's get started.

> *Sous-Chef JOVANNI puts his cap back on, dons an apron with the logo "Cortés School of Imperial Cuisine™," and steps behind the counter of the demonstration kitchen.*

Tonight we are making ... rellenong bangus.

> PROJECTION: [title card]
> Rellenong bangus

6

Rellenong bangus is a traditional Filipino dish ... so this is really exciting for me because Chef Maximo tells me I used to be Filipino! *[handwritten: humour, doesn't know his culture]*

The dish is a specialty of the Bulacan region of the Philippines, but it's enjoyed by all. The Bulakeños apparently have a saying: "Do not eat anything unless it makes you swoon with pleasure." Rellenong bangus has brought pleasure to many people.

Filipinos prepare it on festive occasions – Christmas and other fiestas. So it's a little like a turkey with all the trimmings. And like the Christmas turkey, rellenong bangus is stuffed. *Relleno* is actually the Spanish word meaning ... "stuffed"! And the flavours of this dish very much reflect the Spanish presence in Filipino culture. *[handwritten: colonization? / the name of the dish tells of Spanish influence in the Philippines]*

Chef Maximo has added some of his own personal touches to the dish that reflect his mastery of Imperial Cuisine™. I'll share all his secrets with you over the next hour. *[handwritten: seems very controlling?]*

Well, not *all* because I don't want the master to burn me with a crème brûlée torch again. I'm just kidding ... that last time was just an accident ...

Sous-Chef JOVANNI flinches, recalling the pain.[4]

---

[4] I was hesitant to get too prescriptive with the stage directions in this printed text. The truth is that A Taste of Empire is essentially a clown show and it must have an improvisational feel, especially: (1) in the transitions between chapters where you often have to tidy up or bring in new ingredients; (2) while cooking when you really can't anticipate with exact precision how long an action will take.

So at this point in the play, I probably flinched during most performances. But on other occasions, I might've reassured an audience member who looked aghast. On other occasions, I might've laughed with the audience if they were laughing (that did actually happen from time to time).

Basically, imagine a hilarious ending to this scene because I nailed the transition every single time.

Part 3

DAGUPAN'S RISING TIDE

Sous-Chef JOVANNI stands in front of a cutting board draped with a tea towel.

First, let me introduce you to the star of our show.

Sous-Chef JOVANNI lifts the tea towel to reveal a milkfish on the cutting board.

PROJECTION: [live coverage of fish on cutting board]

This is a milkfish (or bangus as it's called in the Philippines). A few hours ago, it looked like this with shiny silver scales.

PROJECTION: [still image]
picture of a bangus with caption:
MILKFISH or BANGUS (*Actinopterygii gonorynchiformes chanidae chanos*)

Then, with a boning knife and kitchen shears, I scaled it and cut off its pectoral and transverse fins.

Now Chef Maximo taught me that the more you personalize your proteins, the more you treat them with respect. And that's why I christened our friend here Bong-Bong.

PROJECTION: [title card]
Bong-Bong

No, I did *not* name him after gun-enthusiast-turned-Filipino-congressman Ferdinand "Bong-Bong" Marcos Jr.

PROJECTION: [still image]
Ferdinand Marcos Jr. holding a gun

8

No, this Bong-Bong is named in honour of Filipino action-star-turned-senator Bong Revilla.

> PROJECTION: [still image]
> Bong Revilla holding a sword

Now I'm going to loosen Bong-Bong's skin from his flesh, first with this mallet and then with my hands.

> Sous-Chef JOVANNI takes a mallet and starts lightly tapping the fish.

> PROJECTION: [live coverage of fish on cutting board]

Notice how I'm not going medieval on poor Bong-Bong here. The last thing we want to do is to break his skin by tapping too hard. *fish is Symbolic*

Chef Maximo says the bangus is one of the national symbols of the Philippines and it plays a vital role in the Filipino diet. And nowhere is bangus more important than on the Gulf of Lingayen in northern Luzon, which also happens to be Bong-Bong's birthplace.

The largest city on the gulf is Dagupan, the bangus capital of the Philippines. *traditional*

Bangus is what has driven the economy of Dagupan for hundreds of years. In the old days, bangus were harvested in the wild in nets cast from boats. And the hard-working people in those boats were members of the Aeta tribe – the legendary fishermen of Dagupan.[5]

he is innaccurately telling the history of others # —though this botched history is easily beleavable

---

5   Okay, I'll come clean. I took huge liberties with facts in this particular section. Call them alternative facts.
    When Talonbooks generously offered to publish this play, I actually almost declined out of fear of being publicly outed and shamed à la Mike Daisey.
    Here's the unvarnished truth:
    (1) The Aeta are a mountainous tribe of Austronesians, not a coastal tribe.

9

Sous-Chef JOVANNI puts down the mallet and starts
rubbing the milkfish with his hands.

For the Aeta, fishing was not just what they did, it was who
they were. Their way of life was one of tribal customs passed
from generation to generation. Honouring the gods of sea
and sky. Thanking the sun for its sustaining glow. Finding
fish just by listening to the rhythm of the waves and the
song of the wind.

Chef Maximo says that's a ridiculously inefficient way
to get your food. Well, thank goodness that's become a
thing of the past. These days, just about any milkfish you
buy is the product of a hatchery or fish farm. Fish farming
is a pretty simple concept. First, you cram all these fertile
fish together, like at a Club Med. Next, you let them breed
like crazy (just like at a Club Med). Then, you reap in the
rewards (like the bartender at a Club Med).

[handwritten left margin: he is insulting the cultural beliefs of others]

[handwritten: how traditions have been altered for profit]

(2) Fish farming was actually widespread in the Dagupan area for many
centuries though not with modern factory-like efficiencies until recently.
Net fishing did, however, take place a long time ago.
The odd thing about *A Taste of Empire* is that although extensive research went
into its creation, there is nothing remotely resembling academic rigour in the
final product.
I have my reasons for conflating and compressing facts and timelines.
If you ever want to hear them, let's discuss it over a beverage (first round's
on you).
At the risk of sounding defensive, I don't think that Sous-Chef Jovanni
should be held to the same standard of truth-telling as a Mike Daisey or John
Oliver or Trevor Noah. There was a conscious choice to blur the line between
fact and fantasy in creating this play for reasons that will become evident.
I have never represented Sous-Chef Jovanni's narrative as lived experience
or documentary. And I think I offer plenty of clues that should prompt the
viewer to question Sous-Chef Jovanni's credibility as an accurate source of
information.
I do, of course, recognize the huge pitfall in taking shortcuts with facts –
like the Romanians who spoke to me in their native tongue, people really want
to believe that anything said on a stage is true.

[handwritten left margin: Themes]

Fish farming's really old. Chef Maximo says the Mayans used fish farms but it's only in the past hundred years that fish farming caught up with the wonders of the industrial age. Some visionary businessmen realized that if you built a ten-thousand-square-foot factory right next to your fish farm, well, then you could process the fish with *huge* economies of scale. Now you could turn your Club Med into something like ... a Super Sandals resort.

PROJECTION: [video]
Super Sandals resort

Boy, I haven't had a vacation in so long ...

Anyway, Bong-Bong here comes from one of these miracles of food technology – the Imperial Seafood Corporation's state-of-the-art bangus processing plant in Dagupan.

And it's at this plant that we meet the last person to handle Bong-Bong. Before I laid my hands on him, the last pair of hands that touched him belonged to a fellow named Piag Ibasan.

PROJECTION: [still image]
Piag

Sous-Chef JOVANNI lays down the fish and turns on the heating element under the bamboo steamer, which has a lid and contains a banana leaf folded in half.

Piag, like Bong-Bong, was born in Dagupan. For most of the past decade, Piag has worked as a junior inspector at Imperial Seafood.

It's no surprise that Piag ended up in the bangus business. He comes from a long line of proud Aeta fishermen.

> Sous-Chef JOVANNI picks up a honing steel and
> begins to sharpen a boning knife.

Now what you've got to understand about the Aeta is that
they're incredibly stubborn people. They do things their way
and nothing can change that. Not Spanish colonialism, not
American imperialism, not Japanese occupation– ... alism.
No matter what, the Aeta desperately cling to their traditions
and refuse to change with the times.

> PROJECTION: [still image]
> Piag's father

But not Piag. Ten years ago, Piag told his father, Istak,
he was rejecting all that touchy-feely sea/sky/sun/wind
worshipping. He was going to work at the processing plant
instead.

> PROJECTION: [back to live coverage of fish on
> cutting board]

> Sous-Chef JOVANNI takes a boning knife and cuts by
> the gills.

I'm just making a small incision right by the gills. You
might see a little blood if you're trying this at home. That's
normal, Chef Maximo says: ¡Coño carajo! It isn't Imperial
Cuisine™ without a little blood.

Now I'll just put this palette knife through this little
hole I made right by the gills and carefully separate Bong-
Bong's flesh from his skin. If I do this correctly, I'll be able
to squeeze out his insides just like squeezing a tube of
toothpaste.

> Sous-Chef JOVANNI works away with a palette knife
> during the following.

I'll bet Istak felt a bit like Bong-Bong here when Piag told
him he was turning his back on the ancient Aeta traditions.
But just take a look at the life Piag was rejecting. A typical

day for Istak meant fifteen hours of gruelling work on a boat that, by all rights, should have fallen apart years ago. And after all that, Istak and family would still have to sell the day's catch to the local shops and restaurants.

Even though Piag and his father are skilled tradesmen, they're reduced to hustling their wares like some common door-to-door salesman.

By the way, this palette knife that I'm using is from the Maximo Collection™ of deluxe kitchen tools.

PROJECTION: [still image]
advertisement for the Maximo palette knife

Contoured handle, sturdy yet flexible vanadium blade, and a lifetime warranty. When you want the best, you want Maximo.

PROJECTION: [back to live coverage of fish on size!
cutting board] they equate w/ meaning
money importance

So Piag and family are peddling their goods. And before Imperial Seafood opened, Istak would get about sixty cents a kilogram for his bangus. Sixty cents! Even though that's outrageously high, Istak barely makes enough to feed his family. their culture is out
of their hands

And what's more, the size of his catch is tiny. Apparently, all the Aeta fishermen put together can't meet the demand of all the villages along the Gulf. New ways are

Well, all that was before Imperial Seafood. Now, better Dagupan has trusted its future not to fishermen but to scientists, accountants, and MBAs. With its patented hatchery biofeedback system, Imperial Seafood is generating *ten thousand* times the yield of the Aeta tribe.

And the price of bangus has dropped from sixty cents a kilo to twenty-three cents. Now all the restaurants and stores can pass on these savings to their customers and take a

The tribe / locals
are hurt economically
by imperialism

bigger profit margin. (Check out Imperial's website for bulk orders and investment opportunities.)

PROJECTION: [still image]
Imperial Seafood's website

With all the fish Imperial Seafood is producing, not only is there enough to feed the Gulf, there's enough to sell throughout the whole country, and even enough to export overseas to people like you.

As Chef Maximo likes to say: *Everybody's a winner!* Well, everybody with the sense to get off old leaky boats.

PROJECTION: [still image] ~~to leave their culture behind~~
Piag's mother

So, thank God for Piag's mother, Mira. She understood that it was foolish to fight the tide of progress. Mira refused to take Piag out of school early and plunk him on a sinking ship. She was so proud when Piag was the first in the family to graduate from high school.

PROJECTION: [still image]
Piag's graduation photo

Mira tried to convince the other Aeta that they couldn't compete with Imperial Seafood.

It's a shame no one would listen to Mira. The tribe would have been spared so many needless premature deaths. ~~blood~~

So thanks to his mother's foresight, Piag worked for nine years at a state-of-the-art, air-conditioned plant. (Okay, the a/c was for the fish, not Piag, but he stayed nice and cool.)

Piag's pay was the same amount each week. He didn't have to worry about the size of his catch or the weather.

Most important, Piag could provide a better life for himself and his wife, Clara.

PROJECTION: [still image]
Piag and Clara's wedding photo

And all Piag had to do was to stand there eight hours a
day and make sure that the bangus that was harvested
fell within the parameters of edibility before it was sent to
be flash-frozen and made its way onto my cutting board.
Hardly back-breaking work.

Sous-Chef JOVANNI snaps the fish's spine.

[handwritten: symbolic breaking him down / apart]

Now we snap his spine ... at his neck ... and at his tail.[6]
    These days, fish inspection is more important than ever
because in order to keep up with demand for their outstanding product, Imperial Seafood has to squeeze more and
more fish into their pens.

Sous-Chef JOVANNI squeezes out the insides.[7]

PROJECTION: [live coverage close-up of fish meat
and guts squeezing out of fish onto cutting board]

And, as you might expect, all that squeezing means each
hatchling is slightly more susceptible to the odd infection
here and there. But Imperial Seafood's team of scientists anticipated this and were prepared with two brilliant
solutions: one, infuse the water with lots of therapeutic anti-
biotics, and two, hire new local quality-control personnel.
    And more jobs is a terrific thing so, once again, thank
you, Imperial Seafood! [handwritten: polluting?]

---

6   What, pray tell, do these ellipses indicate? Are they for dramatic effect? No,
     they're there because snapping a milkfish's spine is harder than you think.
     I don't mean hard in the sense that it requires physical strength. Rather, fish
     spines are remarkably supple – imagine trying to break a licorice Twizzler by
     bending it. [handwritten: hard work that is overlooked]

7   This is as disgusting as it sounds – like John Hurt in *Alien* disgusting. It never
     ceases to amaze me that people willingly sample the dish after witness~~~ ~~

Piag and his family enjoy comforts his father never dreamed of. And you enjoy cheap and plentiful fish. Before Imperial Seafood entered the market, you couldn't even get Filipino bangus at your local grocery. Everybody's a winner!

Pause. Cheapened fish

Except for Bong-Bong ... and Piag's father ... I think what Chef Maximo meant is everybody who's smart is a winner. Everybody who survives. undermining others

Anyway – what we have on this board is a lot of tasty bits and some not-so-tasty viscera. So let's just get rid of the extra bits, the unwanted scraps – there's liver ... and heart ... Piag's father ... intestine ... environmental regulations ... and that looks like swim bladder ... and now we're left with this beautiful fish meat and about three hundred tiny little fish bones.

We could pick out the bones right now if we had an army of small children with tweezers but your labour laws seem to frown on that so, instead, we'll partially cook the meat. Most recipes call for parboiling, but Chef Maximo just hates the thought of wasting all those juices. So what the master does is to steam the fish meat in a banana leaf to retain its natural succulence.

> *Sous-Chef JOVANNI lifts the lid of the bamboo steamer and unfolds the banana leaf. He places the fish meat in the bottom half of the leaf, folds the top half back over, and replaces the lid.*

Remember, we don't want to fully cook the meat. We just want to firm up the flesh a little bit to make it easier for the sous-chef to pick out the bones. (That's what I used to do for Chef Maximo.)

Right now, I'm doing something really cool – I'm turn-ing Bong-Bong inside out[8] so we can clean him up a bit. And we're going to give him a little shave.[9] See all those tiny bones sticking out? Well, we wouldn't want you to choke on them and die.

~~I'm just kidding. It's okay if you choke. We're insured.~~[10]
Now we turn him back like this. Carefully. Ta-dah![11]

JOVANNI carefully restores Bong-Bong the right away around.

Okay, we're ready for the next part.

Sous-Chef JOVANNI heads to the sink.

not concerned abt anyone unable to afford modern safeties

---

8   What? What the hell do you mean "I'm turning Bong-Bong inside out"?!
It's basically what it sounds like, and it's not that difficult to do. Once you've evacuated the flesh and bones from a fish skin, it's pretty much like a sock. A really gross, slimy sock with a fish head attached. Turning a fish skin inside out requires a little more care than a sock, however, because there are sharp bones protruding where the fins are and you don't want to catch and tear the skin on these bony processes.

9   Once you've got Bong-Bong inside out, "a little shave" means grabbing kitchen shears and trimming all the bones that are sticking out.

10   What's that, you forgot to get insurance? Bad luck for you, bubbeleh.

11   If you turn Bong-Bong right side out with a little swag, you will, in fact, get some applause. What you have just done to a fish is very likely a brand new experience for your audience.

Sous-Chef Jovanni (and Bong-Bong)

Part 4

PUTTING THINGS IN THEIR PLACE

Sous-Chef JOVANNI calls for NEHA.

Neha!! Chop-chop!!

*NEHA, wearing an apron and commis cap, enters.
As Sous-Chef JOVANNI washes his hands, NEHA
clears the fish prep station and sets up the vegetable
prep station.*

This is Neha, the number two sous-chef. When Chef
Maximo found her, she was harvesting kidneys in the streets
of Helsinki.[12] (*to NEHA*) Don't just stand there, make yourself
useful for a change! Move, you waste of space![13]

 (*back to audience*) Oh no, she loves it when I talk to her
like that. That's how Chef Maximo mentored me ... and look
where I am. So now that my assistant is in its proper place
in the backroom, we can make our marinade. I'll start with

---

12   I actually only used this line once or twice in performance. As a running gag,
      I would try to invent a new absurd back story every night – feral lumberjack,
      Bulgarian CrossFit champion, failed theatre critic – whatever came to mind.
          I also wasn't above pandering to my crowd: "She was a grant writer for a
      mid-sized theatre company" always got a laugh (since 80 percent of the people
      who watch theatre also work in theatre) as did "master's candidate in urban
      planning" when I performed at UBC.

13   These are pretty mild examples of what should be ad libbed abuse. Nothing is
      off limits when abusing the assistant onstage; taunts about personal appear-
      ance, ethnic slurs, threats of deportation are all fair game.
          There are really only three guidelines to abusing your Neha: (1) the abuse
      should get progressively worse; (2) push the envelope as far you can (Derek
      Chan did this far more successfully in performance than I ever did); (3) if you
      flash the audience an innocent, impish grin and shrug after hurling abuse, they
      will forgive you even the most vile insults.

this soy sauce ... next, the juice of half a lemon ... some salt and pepper ... and finally, we'll give Bong-Bong a little bath.

Sous-Chef JOVANNI does all.

So our skin is marinating, and our fish is steaming. It's time to set up our *mise en place*. This is the culinary term we chefs use for preparing ingredients – chopping, cutting, measuring – just before the point of cooking. *Mise en place* roughly translates into putting everything in its proper place.

There are lots of ways to make rellenong bangus. Every family has its own recipe – not Chef Maximo's recipe, mind you, but their own. But what you will find in every single version – including the master's – is garlic, onions, and tomatoes sautéed in olive oil.

Sous-Chef JOVANNI turns on the heating element under the sauté pan.

Maybe that sounds familiar? Well, if you do any Spanish cooking, you'll know that this combination is called *sofrito*, and it's the flavour base for many dishes.

PROJECTION: [live coverage close-up of Sous-Chef JOVANNI chopping]

In fact, other than the soy sauce in the marinade, none of the ingredients in this dish are what you would normally think of as being especially Asian. And yet, Chef Maximo says: *Rellenong bangus is quintessentially Asian, a signature dish of the Philippines.*

So how did these Spanish flavours come to define a Filipino dish? The answer begins in 1521.

It was in that year that, under the flag of Spain, the great explorer Ferdinand Magellan landed upon a cluster of seven thousand beautiful islands in the South China Sea. Magellan claimed this fertile land for the glory of Spain and its monarch, Philip the Second.

PROJECTION: [sequence of title cards]
Philip / Philippines / Get it?

Sous-Chef JOVANNI starts to mince garlic.

Unfortunately, many of the indigenous people who happened to be there weren't ready to accept Spain's generous
offer of civilization. Remember those stubborn old Aeta?
Well, these folks[14] were even worse.

And it was their stubbornness that forced Spain to cull
thousands of lawless natives in order to keep the peace and
to bring them into the modern world, just as Spain had
done with the backward savages of the Americas thirty years
earlier.

When the Spanish arrived, indigenous farmers had this
inefficient system where each family used its land to grow
food to feed themselves. They didn't know about cash crops,
storing surpluses, or commodities trading.

Well, Spain soon corrected that. For the benefit of the
farmers, Spain took over their land and taught them the
marvels of modern agriculture. No more growing cassava or
yam to feed their kids. Instead the land was to be used the
way God intended – to create wealth.

The Spanish taught the natives how to grow profitable
crops like sugar cane, tobacco, and coffee, and soon money
was flowing (all the way back to Spain).

Now I know some of you smarty-pants are thinking: hey,
you can't eat tobacco! But the Spanish had already thought
of that and, in exchange for their crops, provided the

---

14   "These folks" would have actually been a thriving settlement in Mactan, an
island in the Visayas. In the Battle of Mactan in 1521, the native forces led by
Datu (Chief) Lapu-Lapu successfully resisted Magellan's expedition and held
off Spanish colonization for about forty years. Coincidentally lapu-lapu is also a
Filipino name for a kind of grouper. Even more coincidentally, lapu-lapu is an
excellent substitute for bangus in this dish.

farmers with the chance to buy food. All at a low cost. Plus a little extra for shipping and handling.

And since the farmers found that lots of caffeine and cigarettes helped keep them alert in the fields, they were able to buy back the coffee, sugar, and tobacco that they grew. Plus a little extra for refining the raw material.

And Spain even allowed the farmers to squat on their former land in exchange for tending the fields. Plus a little extra for rent and supplies.

I hear some of you thinking: hey, that sounds like a lot of extras. But Chef Maximo teaches us: *Every valuable lesson comes at a price.* And he's right. I mean, it wasn't fun that time when the master locked me in the walk-in freezer overnight but now, I never forget to close the freezer door.

So there were a few sacrifices for the Filipinos, but think of all the gifts they got in return.

Like the gift of eternal salvation. Spanish priests stripped the islanders of all their nutty false idols and taught them the love of our one true saviour, Jesus Christ.

And with that came the gift of Christian modesty. Instead of running around half-naked in see-through piña cloth, Spain gave the islanders clothing made from sturdy cottons and thick Spanish wools designed specifically for the tropics.

And, of course, Spain bestowed the gift of their cuisine. *Adobo, guisado, caldereta ... sofrito.* So *that's* how Spanish flavours came to define a Filipino dish.

You know what's funny, though? Although *sofrito* is a flavour we identify as Spanish, none of its ingredients actually come from Spain. Just as Spain spread so many blessings throughout its empire, so too did they receive blessings from earlier empires.

The garlic, onion, and olive oil all originated in Central Asia and were introduced into the Iberian Peninsula around 2000 BCE, probably by one of the great seafaring empires – the Phoenicians, the Greeks, or the Carcinogens.

So here we thought that rellenong bangus was an Asian dish with European ingredients, when all the ingredients were Asian to begin with.

*Sous-Chef JOVANNI picks up a tomato and
starts chopping.*

All except this. The tomato is native to South and Central America. The first domesticated variety was grown in Central Mexico by the Aztecs. Many species of tomatoes were present throughout the continent by the time Columbus landed and Spain civilized the Mayans, Aztecs, and Ninjas.

At first, the Spaniards were afraid that this New World fruit was poisonous. (Or maybe they thought it would turn them red like all those Aztecs!)

But after a while they saw that their loyal subjects in the Philippines weren't dying (or turning red), so they figured it was probably safe to give it a try. So this tomato we think of as "Spanish" comes from an American seed that was transplanted both to Asia and to Europe.

The story of the tomato is the story of the wonders of empire. Only by commanding a vast realm spanning three continents and having the power of life and death over millions of vassals could Spain make the tomato such a beloved fruit to so many. Chef Maximo says that's what Imperial Cuisine™ is all about: *Taking all the goodness of the earth and letting the bounties trickle down.*[15]

---

15   When Derek Chan was translating this play into Cantonese, we talked about what exactly we wanted to convey with this phrase.

It was my hope that the reference to Milton Friedman worked in Chinese as well. I asked whether the Cantonese term for trickle-down economics made sense in this context. Fortunately it does.

Sous-Chef JOVANNI puts the onion, garlic, and tomato in the olive oil.

Look at us, we're making a *sofrito*! (*hollering toward offstage*) Neha!!

Sous-Chef JOVANNI ad libs random abuse to hasten NEHA's entrance.[16]

---

16   My very patient editor requested that I give some examples of ad libbed abuse. I've resisted doing this for two reasons:

    (1) Abuse transcribed on a page just isn't as funny as what is delivered in the context of a live performance.

    (2) I have a theory that you, the reader, can imagine far more offensive things yourself.

    I offer the following evidence to support this theory. When Derek Chan performed his translation of the show in Cantonese, we, of course, couldn't provide English translation surtitles for his abuse of his Sous-Sous-Chef Pedro because it was ad libbed every performance. The surtitle monitor simply read "Random abuse directed at Pedro." And yet, night after night, non-Chinese speaking patrons howled with laughter and delight watching Derek scream at poor Pedro in a language that they couldn't understand. What was literally being said didn't matter – just the notion of abuse was enough to amuse people.

    But since I know my dear editor will insist that I provide at least one example, here was one of the more popular ad libs: one night, I managed to summon enough of my high school German to yell "Kommen Sie her! Schnell! Schnell! Schnell!" at full volume toward Neha. For some reason, people got a kick watching a Chinese guy barking orders in German at a South Asian woman. Which I think just further proves my hypothesis.

Part 5

GLOBAL FLAVOURS

*NEHA enters and goes to remove the wok and the
bamboo steamer. Sous-Chef JOVANNI hurls more
abuse until NEHA exits and begins to pick bones
from the cooked fish meat backstage.*[17] *JOVANNI
smiles innocently to the audience and then returns
his attention to the* sofrito.

We want to cook this mixture over medium-low heat for a
few minutes to let all the rich flavours develop.

While we're waiting on our *sofrito*, let's complete the rest
of our *mise en place*.

PROJECTION: [live coverage of cooking preparation]

To our rich, intense base flavours, we'll add carrot, potato,
and peas.

*Sous-Chef JOVANNI chops carrots and potatoes into
a brunoise.*

Now we know where some of our ingredients originated.
But we don't know where they were grown or where we
bought them. You've probably assumed that all these

---

17   Factoid of no interest to anyone but me: Neha was the only assistant capable
of removing all the bones in the short amount of time available while I did my
shtick onstage. It actually takes a lot of time to remove the three hundred odd
bones in a milkfish. Or more precisely, removing the first 295 bones is really
easy. Getting the final five bones so that no one chokes takes *forever*. Still, Neha
managed to accomplish this.

    For the subsequent runs, we did what is known in cooking demonstrations
as a swap out. We pretended that the sous-sous-chef was picking bones in real
time when, in fact, I had picked bones from a different fish at my own leisure
before the show. You call it cheating; I call it the magic of theatre.

ingredients came from downstairs in the market. But Imperial Cuisine™ embraces a different philosophy from the current, trendy "locavore," "farm-to-table" craze.

Imperial Cuisine™ is all about bold, powerful flavours. No farmers were hugged in the creation of this dish. Why limit ourselves to produce from twenty feet away when we can take advantage of the best ingredients the world has to offer? And that is why we buy all our produce from leading grocery chains like MaxiMart™.

PROJECTION: [still image]
MaxiMart™ ad

Since we bought this garlic at a MaxiMart™, the odds are good it comes from China, which grows almost 80 percent of the world's garlic. One of the ways they've so impressively dominated this market is through their International Garlic Visibility Enhancement Program in tandem with their Domestic Agricultural Worker Pacification Program, which some mean-spirited critics like to call dumping.

Chef Maximo likes to call these critics *pendejos*. I mean, what is there to criticize? Call it dumping – heck, you could call it killing baby pandas – it doesn't change the fact that it's the best thing that ever happened to the working man.

At some hipster organic stand, one bulb of garlic grown on a farm an hour away could cost as much as a dollar fifty. But buy that exact same bulb of garlic (more or less) at a supermarket and it'll cost just twenty cents. (As little as ten cents this week at MaxiMart™!) Now I know there are some granola-crunchers who would love to pay fifteen times more for their food. But doesn't it make more sense to save your hard-earned money?

And what is it that makes Chinese garlic such an outstanding bargain? The miracle of this so-called dumping. China subsidizes its farmers so they can sell us more of their high-quality garlic for less than it costs them to produce. Isn't that great?!

China's way more efficient at subsidizing garlic than some local farmer, so China should be growing all the garlic and the local farmer should stick to running his bed and breakfast.

Normally, Chef Maximo disapproves of things like subsidies. He always says: *¡Puñeta! Government doesn't solve problems – government is the problem.*[18] But the master does make two exceptions for government action: one, lowering the cost of food, and two, creating hotlines to report barbaric cultural practices.[19]

---

18   Of course Chef Maximo is a fan of the Great Communicator. Here, Chef Maximo is paraphrasing one of the more memorable sound bites from Ronald Reagan's first inaugural address on January 20, 1981.

19   This "barbaric cultural practices" line was really funny in November 2015. (Okay, it was mildly amusing.) It referred to an initiative proposed by then Canadian cabinet ministers Kellie Leitch and Chris Alexander to provide a tip line where you could report on all those scary people in turbans and niqabs.

At the play's premiere in June 2010, this line was "building artificial lakes to impress foreign dignitaries" and it did, in fact, get a big laugh. It referred to the Harper government's decision to spend $2 million to build an artificial indoor lake (complete with Muskoka chairs) near the Gardiner Expressway for the G20 summit in Toronto.

As a long aside, I have to say that performing this particular play during the G20 protests was one of the more surreal experiences of my life. I distinctly recall our stage manager Joanna Barrotta arriving later than usual before a preview performance. She looked ashen, having just made the short trek from Spadina Avenue and Front Street to the St. Lawrence Market where we were performing. Along the way she had witnessed a burning police car and protestors battling with police clad in full tactical gear. Toronto had never experienced anything like this – not even during the 1992 Rodney King riot.

With the maelstrom just blocks away from the market, I remember simultaneously feeling: (1) that we were delivering a timely and important examination

Sous-Chef JOVANNI adds the brunoise (carrot and potato) and peas to the sauté pan.

So this garlic was grown in China. So were these onions and carrots – China is also a world leader at subsidizing those farmers. The peas were purchased frozen in a bag with the label "Made in Canada."

PROJECTION: [live coverage close-up of "Made in Canada" label on bag of frozen peas]

Some packaging laws encourage companies to buy their food from anywhere in the world, package it here with some Canadian content, and proudly label it "Made in Canada." So, in this case, the only thing you know for sure was made in Canada is the bag. If you're ever on a Hundred-Mile Packaging Diet, look for this label to ensure your bag-maker is local.

So we really have no idea where these peas are from. In this one bag, these peas might be from three or four different countries. But that's the way we like it. In Imperial Cuisine™, we want to scour the four corners of the earth to bring you the best.

And now, we add our final ingredients to the pan. First, this partially steamed fish minus all the bones.

---

of globalization; and (2) that our little skit was utterly meaningless in the face of people being clubbed with batons and pepper-sprayed.

But back to the topical jokes. In 2016, for Derek Chan's Cantonese version at Gateway Theatre, we changed the line to "shutting down public schools," a reference to the policies of Christy Clark's provincial government in British Columbia. Basically, the line should be a topical reference to any recent action of a sitting government that Chef Maximo would approve of but that the majority of us lefty-leaning theatre lovers would probably find wasteful, stupid, or just flat-out cruel. As I am writing this, the Trump administration has just tabled a federal budget increasing defence spending but cutting, among other things, the National Endowment for the Arts, the Corporation for Public Broadcasting, Meals on Wheels, and meal subsidies for poor schoolchildren. Somewhere in his fortified bunker, Chef Maximo is having an orgasm.

NEHA enters with the deboned fish meat.

Neha, could it have taken you any longer to get all those bones out?[20]

Sous-Chef JOVANNI ad libs random abuse.
NEHA exits.

Next, I'm going to add some raisins, which add some sweetness, and I'll balance that with the master's special combination of tamarind paste, tomato paste, and Worcestershire sauce.

Up until the late 1800s, Filipino cuisine was a fusion of indigenous and Spanish cookery. And then, at the turn of the century, Filipinos saw a whole new empire emerge and a new world of flavour open up to them.

PROJECTION: [still image]
photo from the Spanish-American War

This, of course, would be the American Empire. By 1898, Spain saw its empire in decline.

And in the Spanish-American War, they deservedly got their fat tushies kicked by the lean and buff Yankee forces led, in part, by action-hero-turned-president, Teddy Roosevelt.

PROJECTION: [still image]
photo of Teddy Roosevelt in hunting garb

Although the Americans only officially ruled for a half-century, they had a profound and lasting effect on Filipino culture and cuisine. With their Filipino brothers,

---

20   Again, this line was rarely used in performance. Usually, around this point in the play, I was threatening to call Immigration (none of my three onstage assistants were white so this line tended to elicit gasps and laughs). As the Neha abuse progresses, the laughter should go from the ha-ha variety to the nervous variety to possible uncomfortable silence. Riding the edge of taste and public decorum is actually quite exhilarating.

America shared its love of delicious processed food and convenience food chock full of yummy salt, sugar, and fat. Stuff like this.

Sous-Chef JOVANNI pulls out a can of Spam.

Many of you foodie types scoff at Spam. Mystery meat in a can. Well, there's no mystery to it.

PROJECTION: [still image]
diagram of Spam processing

It couldn't be clearer.

Sous-Chef JOVANNI turns the can over and the
Spam schlorps its way out of the can and onto the
cutting board.

So thanks to the Americans, Filipinos now *love* Spam. And so do we Romanian orphans. And orphans all around the world. Mmm ... just smell that smoky goodness. That looks really, really ...

Sous-Chef JOVANNI picks up the hunk of Spam and
bites into it.[21]

By coincidence, Spam is one of those ingredients that Filipinos like to add to their rellenong bangus now.

---

21   To answer one of the most-asked questions about this piece: yes, I actually like Spam. Way more than I should. Hey, I'm Asian so I'm genetically predisposed to loving the stuff. That said, eating it cold right from the can is not my preferred Spam delivery method.

As you probably guessed, this play draws huge inspiration from Stephen Colbert's former Comedy Central show *The Colbert Report*. Along with being a truly brilliant and fearless satirist, one of the things I admire about Colbert is that the man will eat *anything* to get a laugh. If you don't believe me, go to YouTube and look up "Stephen Colbert eating supercut." Chomping into cold Spam is my homage to the master.

*Sous-Chef JOVANNI playfully pretends to add the
whole block of partially eaten Spam to the sauté pan
but doesn't.*

(*referring to the Spam*) Mmm, this is so good.
   Along with this heavenly Spam, Americans also brought
in other popular brands like this.

*Sous-Chef JOVANNI pulls out a bottle of
Heinz ketchup.*

And nowadays Filipinos like ketchup as a condiment
for their rellenong bangus. (Hey, I bet it'd go really good
with ...)

*Sous-Chef JOVANNI is about to squeeze the ketchup
onto the Spam but stops himself.*

Sorry about that. It's just ... Spam takes me back to all those
Christmas dinners at the orphanage.

*Sous-Chef JOVANNI returns the Spam to its can and
sets it aside; then clears away the ketchup.*

Along with these delicacies, the Americans also introduced
authentic homegrown dishes like spaghetti and pizza. The
popularity of Western fast food in the Philippines exploded.
   And so have Filipino waistlines.

PROJECTION: [title card]
15 percent of the adult population have been
diagnosed as having diabetes or being borderline

And occurrences of people complaining about minor com-
plications like blindness and fainting spells.

PROJECTION: [title card]
Five hundred new cases of diabetes are diagnosed
every day

Fortunately for Filipino diabetics, there's relief in sight.

> PROJECTION: [title card]
> Introducing GlucoMax

Sous-Chef JOVANNI pulls out a vial of insulin.

This is GlucoMax, the Maximo brand of premium insulin.[22] Made from the finest natural ingredients, GlucoMax is proven to decrease your chances of chronic renal failure or a diabetic coma by up to 11 percent.

What I have here is GlucoMax-FL, a variety genetically engineered for Filipinos. It provides safe and effective relief and adds zip to your *adobo*.

> PROJECTION: [title card]
> Warning: Do not take GlucoMax with food

Now some of you diabetics are probably thinking: Hey, that GlucoMax-FL sounds pretty sweet – sure wish I was Filipino. Well, not to worry – no matter where you're from, the GlucoMax family of fine products has a type of insulin that's right for you.

---

22   I really wrestled with whether to cut the GlucoMax section because it's so broad and ludicrous even by the standards of this show. That said, the bit always amused Guillermo and me so we left it in. Some of the show's reviews criticized its "cheesy" qualities, and I'm fairly sure the GlucoMax section contributed to that perception.

   I felt a little vindicated when, in 2012, the Southern chef Paula Deen, famous for her unapologetically unhealthy style of cooking: (1) announced that she had Type 2 Diabetes; (2) signed on as a spokesperson for Victoza, a Novo Nordisk medication for diabetics; (3) continued to cook dishes on air laden with butter and sugar despite her condition. I remember emailing Guillermo and saying, "It's GlucoMax!"

   The GlucoMax / Paula Deen incident taught me never to presuppose anything as too ludicrous – reality will always have the last laugh. Sadly, I relearned this lesson in painful fashion on November 8, 2016 – U.S. Election Day.

PROJECTION: [title card]
Exceptions: Norwegians, Laotians, and Uzbeks

So eat whatever you want, whenever you want. GlucoMax is
there for you when your pancreas isn't.
Okey-dokey, it looks like we're done here.

*Sous-Chef JOVANNI gazes at the sauté pan in
admiration.*

Part 6

BEAUTIFUL

Sous-Chef JOVANNI reaches for the sauté pan.

I should probably take that pan off the heat. And now we let this all cool down before we stuff it back into Bong-Bong. This will take a few minutes but we're not just going to sit around idly and wait. As Chef Maximo likes to say: *A lazy sous-chef is like Chantilly cream: they both improve with whipping.*

So while our stuffing is cooling, we have time to make a garnish for our plate.

Sous-Chef JOVANNI hones a paring knife.

Some people consider edible garnish a little passé. Trends keep changing. In the sixties, a plate that looked like this might have been considered quite chic at any get-together.

PROJECTION: [still image]
photo from a 1960s cookbook

Today, a fine dining plate is more likely to look like this – (*refers to projection*).

PROJECTION: [still image]
photo of a molecular gastronomy plate

Chef Maximo always laughs and says whoever made that plate is a real ... what was that word, again? ... oh yeah, a real *maricón*. Yeah, I don't know what that means, either.

But Chef Maximo doesn't really care what the current trend is ... because the master transcends trends. He says that vegetable garnishes add colour and as well as visual and textural contrast. So if that's what the master wants, that's what we're going to do.

Unfortunately, I don't have anywhere near the knife skills of Chef Maximo. Among his many other gifts, the master is easily the greatest garnish chef since Marie-Antoine Carême himself.

Maybe you've heard of Carême? He was the father of French Cuisine and, during the French Revolution, the most celebrated chef in the world. Basically, he was the Chef Maximo of the late 1700s.

Carême was famous for his incredible *pièces montées*, these statuary centrepieces made out of sugar, pastry, and marzipan. I know that Carême was one of Chef Maximo's inspirations when he invented Imperial Cuisine™ – maybe some of you saw his exhibition where he recreated some of Carême's most famous *pièces montées*? If not, I have some pictures from the catalogue. Let's take a look – (*refers to projection*).

> PROJECTION: [still image]
> *replica of a Carême centrepiece*

Isn't that incredible? To have one genius replicate the work of another genius? I read all about Carême and this period in French history when I wrote Chef Maximo's bestselling book on Carême called *Genius on Genius* (available at chef maximo dot com).

> PROJECTION: [still image]
> *another replica of a Carême centrepiece*

I remember that Carême first made this centrepiece in 1788 right after this very harsh winter that destroyed French wheat crops. Chef Maximo says it was a blessing that the peasants had this work of art to lift their spirits when they were starving.

> PROJECTION: [still image]
> *final replica of a Carême table spread*

Oh! This is Carême's masterpiece. Can you believe that's nothing more than sugar and almonds? This was originally made for a very famous feast celebrating the cream of French society. Um ... I wish I could remember the date ... all I remember is that it was on the same night that there were those unfortunate bread riots in Paris ... and that the main courses were pheasant, then lobster, then a *capon ballotine*. But the meal wouldn't have been the same without that beautiful centrepiece. So let's make a garnish ...

Sous-Chef JOVANNI washes his hands.

This is the part of the demonstration where Chef Maximo dazzles you with some vegetables and a knife. But I'm going to do something a little more modest – a tomato rose. It's a simple and elegant garnish. It's actually one of the first things Chef Maximo taught me when I was a little boy. Right after he taught me the proper way to force-feed a goose for foie gras ...

PROJECTION: [live coverage of Sous-Chef JOVANNI carving a tomato rose]

Sous-Chef JOVANNI carves in awkward silence for quite a while, then finally speaks.

This is where Chef Maximo juggles cleavers while singing "La Colegiala" ... yeah, it's as cool as it sounds.

Sous-Chef JOVANNI timidly sings a few bars of "La Colegiala."

Oh boy, what now? ... Hey, I can tell you something about this tomato. Yeah, I can do that. Just like the master would. I can do this.

Sous-Chef JOVANNI clears his throat and starts to clumsily improvise a story.

Now let us meet the last person to handle this tomato. Before I laid my hands on it, the last pair of hands that touched him belonged to a Mexican migrant worker named Carlos Ramirez.

PROJECTION: [still image]
photo of Carlos

His is a tale of intrigue and suspense and ... uh ... tomatoes.

Singing a mournful ranchera to the lonely Mexican moon, Carlos's perilous journey begins as he crosses the border under the cover of nightfall. He stares out at the starless sky, squishes himself up with more than a dozen fellow Mexicans, and leaves his family behind for yet another season. Carlos, who picked this tomato, is fifty years old but looks and feels much, much older – he's made this desperate crossing more times than he can remember.

When he arrives, Carlos, who picked this tomato, finds himself in cramped quarters with five other workers. He's a big man but he sleeps on a tiny, dirty, old mattress. There's no shower – they use a tap and some buckets for bathing.

PROJECTION: [still images or video sequence]
photos of migrant workers' housing conditions

His working conditions aren't much better. Carlos wants to do something about the living and working conditions but he doesn't know how. He can't form a union because that's against the law.

So Carlos, who picked this tomato, lies on his old mattress and counts the days until he can return to his wife, Teresa, and their two daughters, Lumi and Maribel.

Sous-Chef JOVANNI shows the audience his completed rose.

That wasn't so bad, was it? There we go. We'll just save that dear little rose for our finished platter. How are we doing?

Sous-Chef JOVANNI checks on the sauté pan.

Okay, that still needs a few minutes to cool down so let's put these nasty, dirty things out of sight.

> *Rather than saving it, Sous-Chef JOVANNI cavalierly discards the unused innards of the tomato and then starts to tidy.*

That Carlos, he seemed like a really nice guy. He showed me a picture of his little girls – they're so cute. The youngest one, Maribel, has diabetes, and they don't have GlucoMax in his village back home. That's why Carlos has to keep coming here every year.

Oh yeah, Carlos isn't in California – he's right here in Ontario, just a few hours away. When I told you Carlos travelled under the cover of night? He took a red-eye flight because it was cheaper. And the part where he was squished up with a dozen other workers? They flew Air Canada and, you know, there's hardly any leg room in economy (even for a Mexican).

So I met Carlos downstairs in the market, where he was helping his owner.[23] I was supposed to buy the tomatoes at MaxiMart™ but I couldn't because Neha forgot to remind me.

---

23   On page 100 of Alia Ziesman's master's thesis, "'Will Work for Food': Canada's Agricultural Industry and Recruitment of South East Asian Temporary Migrant Workers," presented to the University of Guelph in May 2013, a migrant worker named Wendy says, "Sometimes I have to go to clean my owner's farmhouse too, sometimes they call me to go clean house." Though "owner" is shorthand for "farm owner," there is something harrowing about this master-slave connotation that I wanted to incorporate into Sous-Chef Jovanni's vocabulary.
      Here is another reference to "my owner": CBC News reported on September 10, 2014, the death of Ivan Guerrero, a temporary foreign worker who drowned in May on the Ormstown, Quebec, farm where he worked. "*Es como si fuera yo ... un perro,*" he had said of his boss. "It's like I'm the dog, and she's my owner."

I got to talking with Carlos when his owner went back to the truck for a bit. Yeah, and it sounds like he's got it pretty hard. So I tell Carlos, "You thinking picking tomatoes is tough? Try scaling fish locked up in a freezer overnight." Yeah, we had a good laugh. What a great guy ...

But later I got to thinking, maybe Carlos shouldn't complain so much. Sure, his job is tough, but at least he's got one. If people are lining up for your job, how bad can it be? At least that's what the master tells me whenever I'm crying after a triple shift.

So I don't think Carlos should be saying all that stuff. It seems really ungrateful.

And it's kind of ungrateful to all of you after everything you've done for Carlos. He wouldn't even be here without the Seasonal Agricultural Workers Program.

> *PROJECTION: [still image]*
> *close-up of text of first few sections in Seasonal*
> *Agricultural Worker Program regulation*

Thanks to the SAWP, Carlos enters your country legally. So he's not like all those illegal criminals Donald Trump keeps talking about.[24] He's here because you made a place for him.

And thanks to your generosity, Carlos gets to do a job that none of you want to do. He can buy medicine for his daughter. You can buy cheap and plentiful tomatoes. Everybody's a winner!

---

24   In 2010, before the bewildering rise of the Orange One, this line read "like all those illegal criminals in Arizona," a reference to some of the draconian deportation laws being proffered by Arizona Governor Jan Brewer at the time.

    If this text is to be performed ten years from now, I'm fairly confident you'll be able to replace this Trump reference with some new demagogue fomenting anti-immigrant hysteria.

Sous-Chef JOVANNI goes to check on the cooked fish mixture.

I think our fish has cooled down. Neha!!

Sous-Chef JOVANNI ad libs even more abuse of NEHA until she enters.

Part 7

LAW AND SAUSAGES

NEHA enters with prepared ingredients for the next cooking segment. Even nastier abuse follows until NEHA exits.

PROJECTION: [live coverage of cooking preparation]

We'll just add bread crumbs to help bind our mixture together.

Sous-Chef JOVANNI does so and then turns on the heating element under the large pan.[25]

Bong-Bong has been waiting so patiently and now we'll put all this delicious stuffing back into him. You could use a long-handled spoon to do this. But Chef Maximo likes to use a piping bag.

---

[25] This is one of the more important stage directions in the whole piece. The large pan (the only pan we could find that was large enough for a whole fish was a paella pan) holds about a litre of canola oil in which you eventually shallow-fry the whole battered fish.

It takes a bit of time to get 4 cups (1 litre) of cooking oil to maintain a steady temperature of 350 degrees Fahrenheit.

For one performance, I forgot to preheat the pan with the oil. When I got to the part where I have to fry Bong-Bong – which incidentally is just about the only part of the show that's not supposed to be funny – the oil was still at room temperature. I was forced to ad lib for about 7–8 minutes while the oil was heating up. In stage terms, this is an eternity – I'm pretty sure I was telling knock-knock jokes by the end. It was a rather brutal experience for me and, I imagine, for the invited guests. Fortunately, it happened on dress-rehearsal night and for each subsequent performance, Joanna Barrotta, stage manager extraordinaire, placed a bright yellow Post-it with the single word "OIL!" right next to the ramekin with the bread crumbs. There are certain mistakes you only make once.

Sous-Chef JOVANNI fills a piping bag with the cooled
fish-meat mixture.

What I'm doing might seem familiar to those of you who
have made your own sausage. That's all rellenong bangus
is, essentially – a fish sausage. But instead of using any old
sausage casing, the fish skin becomes its own casing. How
cool is that?

Legend has it that rellenong bangus was invented in the
mid-nineteenth century.[26] In Bulacan, there was a renowned
Spanish surgeon who was also an accomplished hunter,
fisherman, and taxidermist. One day, his Filipina cook
helped him stuff a giant lapu-lapu for his display case. And
after that, she was inspired to create rellenong bangus. Or,
so the story goes.

But Chef Maximo says that the odds of a Filipino woman
inventing something so brilliant are about the same as finding a Jew at his country club.

Okay, now we'll pipe this mixture through the hole by
Bong-Bong's gills.

Sous-Chef JOVANNI takes the filled piping bag,
places the nozzle into the incision by the gills, and
pipes the fish-meat mixture into the skin casing.

Chef Maximo really likes this quote from Mark Twain:
"Those who respect the law and love sausage should watch
neither being made."

Yeah, I didn't understand it either. I mean, why wouldn't
you want to see sausage being made? There's nothing icky
about this process, is there?

But Chef Maximo says they didn't know any better way
back then. In Mark Twain's day, they'd throw just about any-

---

26   This creation story is a complete fabrication, in case you're wondering. I did try
      to unearth any early accounts or recipes for this dish but came up short. The
      origins of this dish remain a mystery.

thing into a sausage. They weren't as good as we are today at getting rid of unwanted scraps.

PROJECTION: [still image]
diagram of Spam processing

And then the master explained that, back then, they were just as primitive when it came to making laws. When Twain made his little quip, America was in the middle of a foreign war – the Philippine-American War, not to be confused with the Spanish-American War.

PROJECTION: [sequence of title cards]
Or the Mexican-American War / the Korean War / the Vietnam War / etc.[27]

To bring fast food, ketchup, and Spam to the Filipinos, first, America had to sacrifice some of their brave young men to defeat very determined terrorists.

PROJECTION: [title card]
Four thousand American soldiers were killed during the Philippine-American War

---

27   In our productions, these title cards cycled slowly at first, then ramped up in speed until they went by too fast for the human eye to read.

     A list of countries that the United States ventured into as a belligerent or combatant in a war, intervention, or incursion since 1904 would include (but not be limited to): Afghanistan, Albania, Angola, Bolivia, Bosnia, Cambodia, Chile, Colombia, Cuba, the Dominican Republic, Egypt, El Salvador, Greece, Grenada, Guatemala, Haiti, Honduras, Indonesia, Iran, Iraq, Kuwait, Laos, Lebanon, Liberia, Libya, Macedonia, Mexico, Pakistan, Panama, Puerto Rico, Russia, Saudi Arabia, Somalia, Syria, Turkey, Uruguay, Virgin Islands, Yemen, Yugoslavia, and Zaire.

All America wanted to do was to extend the blessings of liberty to their little brown brothers.[28] So, like the Spanish before them, they were genuinely thrown for a loop when the Filipinos rejected their generous offer to take care of them. Fortunately, Americans have always been really good at maintaining law and order.

PROJECTION: [title card]
Estimates of Filipino casualties range from
250,000 to 1 million

One of the earliest methods they had for suppressing rebel insurrection was a technique called the water cure. Take the case of Tobeniano Ealdama, who was captured by Captain Edwin Glenn.[29]

PROJECTION: [back to live coverage of piping]

Ealdama was bound and his mouth was forced open. Salt water was forced down his throat until his stomach became distended. Then, the water was forced out of his belly with the heel of a soldier's boot. When Captain Glenn ordered a

---

28   This charming turn of phrase is an actual term coined by William Howard Taft, the first American Governor-General of the Philippines and later, the twenty-seventh president of the United States. According to American historian Creighton Miller, the phrase reflects a policy of "paternalist racism" promoted by Theodore Roosevelt and was not originally intended to be derogatory or an ethnic slur. I guess it depends on your point of view, eh?

29   Unlike the rellenong bangus myth I created, this horrifying account is all too true. I remember reading about the water cure just as the morality and efficacy of waterboarding was being debated by politicians and pundits. The parallels are incredibly unsettling.

    In fact, many incidents that took place during the Spanish-American War and Philippine-American War bear an eerie resemblance to events from the more recent U.S. invasion of Iraq. For example, the non-existent weapons of mass destruction that prompted aggression in Iraq are reminiscent of the explosion of the U.S.S. *Maine*, the later discredited *casus belli* for war with Spain.

second round, Ealdama confessed the location of five hundred terrorists. And their families. *That* is the water cure.[30]

PROJECTION: [still image]
photograph of water cure

Today, we look at the water cure with a little distaste. It's
hard to believe that our closest allies could have behaved so
crudely. But again, like the master says, they didn't know
any better. They were stuck with the tools they had on hand
because it wasn't until 1912 that cellophane was invented.

Sous-Chef JOVANNI pulls out a box of cling wrap.

After 1912 you could place the cellophane on the face of
the person being questioned. Instead of being drowned, he
would only *think* he was being drowned.

Sous-Chef JOVANNI demonstrates by placing some
cling wrap over his own face while pretending to gasp
for air. Then he removes the cling wrap and giggles.

---

30   This section would not have been possible without the discovery of the "evacua-
      tion" method of preparing rellenong bangus – i.e., making a slit, squeezing out
      the insides, and then restuffing the fish through the slit. I talk more about this
      method in the introduction to my recipe later in this book.
          The juxtaposition of the water cure description alongside the visual of hav-
      ing the fish stuffed and engorged was upsetting for a lot of people.
          Much like the gradually escalating abuse of Neha, the idea behind placing
      this section here was to keep testing the audience's boundaries for what they
      could laugh at.
          I remember a friend telling me afterwards that with the water-cure section
      I had somehow crossed a line; it didn't fit with the tone of the show up to that
      point.
          I didn't disagree that there was a tonal shift but I did gently remind him
      that at this point in the show, my audience had already chuckled as Sous-Chef
      Jovanni cheerfully described the genocide of Indigenous peoples in the Phil-
      ippines, as well as French peasants starving while the aristocracy feasted. So
      it's not so much that material became that much darker – people just stopped
      finding it cute.

So with the invention of this little baby, it became possible to take the cruel, invasive, and immoral water cure and modify it into the safe, effective, and perfectly legal technique we use today – waterboarding.

> PROJECTION: [still image]
> photo of waterboarding with caption:
> "A dunk in the water"—Dick Cheney on
> waterboarding

And, of course, cellophane is also very useful for preserving food. If you add more breadcrumbs to this leftover stuffing and pan fry it, it makes a wonderful fish cake.

> Sous-Chef JOVANNI uses the cling wrap to wrap the
> excess stuffing and washes his hands.[31]

---

31   At the end of this scene, we had planned to close the conversation about Tobeniano Ealdama and Captain Edwin Glenn with a series of projections:

> PROJECTION: [title card]
> Tobeniano Ealdama testified at the court martial of Captain
> Edwin Glenn

> PROJECTION: [title card]
> Captain Glenn was found guilty

> PROJECTION: [title card]
> He was sentenced to a one-month suspension and a fifty-dollar fine

> PROJECTION: [title card]
> Ealdama was convicted as a "war traitor" and sentenced to ten years'
> hard labour

The projections were cut in rehearsals because they didn't really work in the context of performance. Viewers were already reeling from the waterboarding sequence and this epilogue would have been too much.

Part 8

GOLDEN FINISH

Sous-Chef JOVANNI dries his hands.

There, Bong-Bong is looking good as new. We are just moments away from Imperial Cuisine™ ecstasy. At this stage, some recipes call for –

Sound of a cellphone. The ring tone is "The Imperial March (Darth Vader's Theme)" from Star Wars.

Omigosh! That's Chef Maximo calling! I can't believe this, he called! It's the master! Hey, gimme that!

NEHA enters with cellphone, which Sous-Chef JOVANNI snatches from her.

(*into phone*) Chef Maximo! ¡Hola! How are you, master – What's that? Yes, sir ...

(*to audience*) Chef Maximo bids you all an imperial greeting. And he'd like to remind you that all the cookware used tonight is available for purchase at chef maximo dot com.

(*back to phone*) What was th–? I was just about to fry – no, master, I didn't screw it up, I did it just like you taught me, but Neha was absolutely no help at all –

Sorry, sir, what did you say? You –? But – but sir – sir, I don't – I don't understand ... uh-huh ... uh-huh ... I see ... work for less ... I understand ... no, no, of course, whatever you think is best. Thank you, master. (*to* NEHA) He wants to talk to you.

Sous-Chef JOVANNI gives the phone back to NEHA, who exits. Sous-Chef JOVANNI then washes his hands.

So where were we?

Yes, we need to finish this fish, don't we? Most recipes suggest baking it, but Chef Maximo prefers to batter it to give it colour and crunch.

So here we dip our fish in the master's special blend of cilantro, rice flour, garlic, and spices. And we'll coat it in panko bread crumbs. Our oil is nice and hot. And ...

Sous-Chef JOVANNI places the battered bangus into the pan with hot oil.

PROJECTION: [back to live coverage of cooking preparation]

Now we just wait for our bangus to come to a beautiful golden finish. While we wait, we're going to do one last thing: we'll make a quick sauce to add the perfect complement to all our hard work. Our sauce is basically shallots and herbs in a red-wine reduction. What makes this sauce sublime is this –

Sous-Chef JOVANNI pulls out a bottle of wine.

PROJECTION: [still image]
Maximo Rojo ad from the Cortés Estates Winery

Maximo Rojo from the Cortés Estates Winery. This full-bodied red boasts aromas of coffee, berries, and ...

Pause.

We don't need a red-wine reduction. Why would we want to reduce such a nice wine?

Sous-Chef JOVANNI uncorks the bottle and takes a healthy swig. He continues drinking throughout the following.

You remember Piag?

PROJECTION: [still image]
picture of Piag

Remember I told you he was enjoying his great new job at
Imperial Seafood? Well, there's more to his story.

Piag and his wife, Clara, have two boys: Manny and José.

And Piag gets promoted to shift leader. But his promo-
tion doesn't last long because Imperial Seafood shuts down
the plant in Dagupan and moves it to China.

Chef Maximo said he and the other executives at Imperial shut down the plant because they were looking out for
you shareholders.

Yeah, a lot of you are part-owners of Imperial Seafood
through your mutual funds and pensions.

PROJECTION: [still image]
a mutual fund prospectus

So all you owners, of course you want your stake in Imperial
Seafood to grow 5, 10, 15 percent every single year.

So instead of giving Piag and his co-workers raises, you
gave that money to yourselves as dividends. Oh, and you
gave Imperial's executives generous bonuses. Like Chef
Maximo always says: *You feed the body starting at the head.*

But that Piag ... seems he was a stubborn old Aeta after
all. He just wouldn't change with the times. He organized
the workers and threatened to halt production unless they
got raises.

PROJECTION: [still images]
photos of Filipinos on a picket line

And it was this threat that forced you to close the plant. So
Piag really brought this on himself. I mean, my pay hasn't
changed in the past ten years. And I haven't had any time
off (not even after that incident with the crème brûlée
torch) ... but you never heard me whining, because I love

this job ... But if I had complained like Piag (and I never did), the master would've had every right to replace me – Excuse me, I need to flip my fish.

Sous-Chef JOVANNI delicately flips the fish using a spatula.

PROJECTION: [still images of Filipino strikers overlap with live coverage of fish cooking in sauté pan; as the fish is flipped, the still images of Filipino strikers slowly dissolve to black]

So yeah, maybe Piag is out of work, but at least he's got Clara to pick up the slack. She leaves her children with their grandmother so she can come here to Canada to take care of your children.

So, Manny and José get to know their *lola* better, Piag gets to see the Filipino countryside as he looks for work, and you enjoy cheap and plentiful child care. Everybody's a winner ...

Sous-Chef JOVANNI takes one last swig from the bottle.

It seems that this will be my first and last demonstration. Chef Maximo called to inform me that my services are no longer required. Apparently, he promised Bono that he would give aid to three refugees from ... from the latest place. And it turns out that three refugees will work for a little less than what I make. Which I find surprising ... though I suppose I shouldn't.

Excuse me, I'm going to pack a few things.

Sous-Chef JOVANNI gathers his pathetically meagre belongings and packs them into a duffle bag.

You know what's funny? I really loved being up here ... And you ... you've been a fantastic audience. I hope you learned something here tonight. I sure did.

I learned that personalizing your proteins doesn't do shit. Hey, Bong-Bong, how's it going? You comfy in there? Why make anything personal? That Filipina taking care of your kids and that old guy picking your tomatoes and that idiot who cooks your fish? Why did I bother telling you our names? Who cares?

This is the key to Imperial Cuisine™: you get to eat the world. Anything you want is yours – no matter how expensive – because Piag and Carlos and Bong-Bong and me ... we always pick up the bill.

A long pause.

Part 9

OUT OF THE FRYING PAN ...

Then, Sous-Chef JOVANNI looks down at the fish.
He washes his hands and removes the fish using
a spatula.

That looks perfect. We need to let that cool down a bit.
When it's not as hot, we'll just put that on a platter with the
garnishes we made.

I'm sorry about ... all that. I ... I hope I didn't spoil your
appetite. Because this is really, really delicious ...

And I'm sorry I could only make enough portions for a
few of you. (I wish I had more time.) But I'm sure you can
work out who gets to eat; you Canadians are so polite.

Sous-Chef JOVANNI takes off his commis cap, apron,
and chef's jacket.

So ... my job is done. I guess that puts Neha in charge. Well
played, Neha! Well played.

Sous-Chef JOVANNI picks up his duffle bag and
the Spam.

Don't worry about me, I'll be fine. I'm sure the orphanage
will take me back.

Sous-Chef JOVANNI schlorps out the Spam again
into his hand and then turns to address the audience
one last time.

Well, enjoy your little taste of empire.

Sous-Chef JOVANNI takes another bite of Spam.

Aren't you even going to try some? I worked pretty hard,
you know. Come on ...

*Sous-Chef JOVANNI defensively holds his can
of Spam.*

You don't want my Spam too, do you?

*Sous-Chef JOVANNI walks out of the kitchen,
protecting his Spam all the way.*

PROJECTION: [title card]
Bon appétit and good night

THE END

*Playwright's Note: After the bows, tasting samples
of the finished rellenong bangus are served to the
audience.*[32]

---

32   I think the thing I loved the most about doing this show was watching the
      varied reaction of my guests while serving Bong-Bong.
          Some were so deeply affected by what transpired that they would stick
      around afterwards, searching for some kind of shared catharsis, but adamantly
      refusing to eat the bangus.
          Others seemed blithely unaware of the show's political implications and
      gleefully went, "Mmm, that looks yummy!" I'm still not sure whether these
      patrons were truly oblivious or just highly adept at compartmentalizing.
          I appreciate that all reactions are valid. It was never my intention to trau-
      matize my guests so that they wouldn't partake afterwards. I think the show is
      ultimately about saying: here's a dish, here's the real cost of the dish, now you
      decide whether you want to eat.
          For those of you who think I hold those who diffidently consume in harsh
      judgment, you'd be wrong. I've eaten my share of rellenong bangus and then
      some; I'm in no position to cast stones.

Ready to serve Bong-Bong

Playwright's Afterword

My wife calls *A Taste of Empire* my miracle play.

It was May 2010 and rehearsals for the premiere production of *A Taste of Empire* were about to begin. The thing was ... I hated the script. I don't think I was the only one.

Perhaps hate is a strong word but I think it's fair to say that no one, especially myself, was particularly enthused about starting rehearsals. Though my director and collaborator Guillermo Verdecchia never stated it explicitly, I sensed his frustration with the way the draft was (or, more accurately, wasn't) progressing. I imagine that Nina Lee Aquino, then the artistic director of Cahoots Theatre Company, shared Guillermo's concern because she had brought in the formidable Ric Knowles as a dramaturg quite late in a five-year process of development.

I felt particularly bad for Nina because I, as her predecessor at Cahoots, was the one who programmed *A Taste of Empire* for a June 2010 run. In hindsight, it was an act of hubris to program a play that, at the time, was so clearly not ready for production. The thing was I knew that the piece had a winning premise and that much of the material resonated with workshop audiences. Sure, the draft-in-progress still felt repetitive and didactic but, back when I programmed *A Taste of Empire*, I had supreme confidence in my ability to make it work.

The trouble was, by May 2010 that confidence had vanished. In its place were severe clinical depression and crippling writer's block. With rehearsals just around the corner, I found myself sleeping more than fourteen hours a day, unable to cope with basic tasks, and constantly irritable or sad.

It was Chef Maximo who saved me. In earlier drafts of *A Taste of Empire*, the show was a demonstration without the Chef Maximo conceit. It was presented as a straight lecture play with me portraying myself. Before Chef Maximo came into my life, I was quite adamant that I didn't want *A Taste of Empire* to have a plot or characters. For reasons I don't understand now, I held this intractable belief that the piece had to be "authentic" – if I played different characters, or constructed anything other than the reality of me cooking for you in real time, then it somehow wouldn't ring true.

Unfortunately, the "authentic" version of myself was so clearly against unchecked globalization that the play felt more like a cheerless diatribe or, worse, an extended straw man argument. My dish had plenty of salt but little in the way of seasoning.

And then when everything seemed hopeless, I had this vision of Chef Maximo Cortés, the creator-guru of Imperial Cuisine, a culinary movement that was the antithesis of sustainable farm-to-table cuisine. In my mind, Chef Maximo was an amalgam of Gordon Ramsay, Augusto Pinochet, and Dick Cheney with a little P.T. Barnum thrown in for good measure.

The emergence of this culinary-genius-cum-banana-republic despot changed everything. Suddenly my unfocused harangue had a point of view. Suddenly this show that I had dreaded doing was fun again. Most importantly, Chef Maximo begat Sous-Chef Jovanni – the *naïf* clown version of myself.

Instead of Jovanni, the depressive burnout, decrying corporate greed for an hour, the ever-optimistic Sous-Chef Jovanni would be free to gleefully parrot Chef Maximo's neo-conservative dogma. This one modulation to the script turned a dry treatise into an offbeat satire.

And with the Sous-Chef Jovanni persona, I felt free to push the envelope and incorporate edgy material without the fear of alienating my audience. As an unwitting tool of the patriarchy, I was able to make racist and sexist comments, abuse my assistant, and even celebrate the invention of waterboarding. And then, with Sous-Chef Jovanni's pathetic epiphany, I could disavow the hateful philosophy I had just espoused. Finally,

I had found the voice for the play. I had found my voice. My true, authentic voice.

Once Chef Maximo entered the picture, rewrites flowed easily. I smashed through a year of painful writer's block and felt real happiness in the process.

None of this would have happened had I not taken the life-changing step of seeking help for depression and anxiety. After I was diagnosed, treatment soon followed, so it's entirely conceivable that Chef Maximo was a side effect of my new antidepressants. Some people believe that Big Pharma is as evil as Imperial Seafood but, without it, I guarantee you would not be reading this play.

Today, with therapy, medication, and the enduring love of a truly amazing partner, I am proud to say that the good days now far outnumber the bad ones. Creativity returned to my life and so did joy.

And that is why my beloved wife refers to *A Taste of Empire* as a miracle play: something was found when all seemed lost.

But for me, the miracle is not just about personal recovery. (Though if my story encourages even one person in need to seek help, I'll feel one step closer to heaven.) For me, the miracle of this play is that it restored my faith in my vocation.

I had been so caught up in pursuing a *vérité* performance style that I had forgotten basic and obvious tenets of art: sometimes the truth lies in artifice; sometimes invention can be more revelatory than reality.

The invention of Sous-Chef Jovanni, for example, revealed truths about my own personality and was just the tonic I needed at that time in my life. I discovered that this hapless innocent is paradoxically nothing like me and yet very much like me.

And Chef Maximo was an even more potent invention. Maximo Cortés – the gourmand, the destroyer, the bully – personifies so much of what angers and frightens me about the world. By manifesting him as an over-the-top blowhard, I was able to use my art to laugh at my anxiety.

So good old Chef Max was a miracle in many ways. I thank him for saving my play, for helping me on the path to wellness, and for reaffirming my faith that theatre can proclaim the truth and heal the weary soul.

Recipe for Rellenong Bangus
(Stuffed Milkfish)

Serves 10 to 12 (or an entire audience as small tasting plates)

Creating this recipe for rellenong bangus was one of the more pleasurable parts of writing *A Taste of Empire*. It was an interesting process since the method of preparing the dish had to meet four very different criteria:

(1) It had to taste good.

(2) It had to look good.

(3) It had to fit with the themes of the play.

(4) It had to fit with the theatricality and actions of the play.

Two aspects of my show recipe are distinctive: first, the "evacuation" method of emptying and stuffing the fish; and second, the battering and pan-frying to finish the dish.

In early workshops of *A Taste of Empire* (at that time, the play had the working title *Bangus*), I used the much more common method of preparing rellenong bangus – slitting the fish along the belly, scraping out the flesh and bones and discarding the organs, stuffing the sautéed fish meat and seasonings back in the skin, and sewing the fish skin back together with needle and thread.

Then one day, I watched a YouTube video where a woman used what I call the evacuation method: she made a cut and squeezed out the insides just as I describe in the show – like a tube of toothpaste. I was mesmerized by this horrifying and fascinating display and I knew I had to replicate it in the next workshop. After a little practice, I became quite adept at it.

The evacuation method was a definite keeper because of its inherent showiness yet grossness, and because it allowed me to incorporate the highly upsetting action of overstuffing poor Bong-Bong using a piping bag as I described the similar action of the water cure on Tobeniano Ealdama.

The second distinctive Imperial Cuisine™ flourish was the idea of battering and pan-frying the bangus at the end. Most traditional recipes call for baking the dish in an oven after stuffing, but this traditional method has two downsides. First, had I thrown Bong-Bong in a preheated oven, I would have had nothing to do onstage for the next forty minutes. (This is why most cooking shows do a "swap-out" when it's time to put the cake or casserole in the oven and exchange the unbaked item for a perfect example of what it should look like after time in the oven.) Second, baked rellenong bangus is actually not all that attractive. It comes out of the oven looking somewhat brown and rubbery (like a lot of Filipino cuisine, it tastes a lot better than it looks).

I thought that battering the fish would give it a more palatable colour and I was right. At first, I had tried deep-frying the battered fish. It looked and tasted fine but the problem was that the technique was too fast – deep-frying didn't leave me with enough time for anything resembling a denouement to the play. Shallow pan-frying on both sides worked out a lot better.

For the batter, I chose to adapt a Thai-inspired rice flour–based recipe. I figured the combination of garlic, black peppercorns, and fish sauce would make a lovely complement to the savoury flavours of the fish.

Finally, the addition of panko crumbs on top of the batter, as well as adding a crunchy texture and colour, served two very practical purposes: first, it increased the cooking time, which meant I could fit in the material I wanted; and second, it added some structural integrity since the fish head had a habit of falling off with just batter alone. After I dredged the battered fish in panko, it added that extra bit of rigidity to avoid the embarrassment of fish decapitation at the end of the show.

Perhaps the loveliest compliment I've received from patrons afterwards is that the dish reminds them of the rellenong bangus their mothers used to make. It means a lot to me because I've strayed so far from any traditional recipe. I'm fairly sure no one's mother ever used a Thai-influenced batter and Japanese-style bread crumbs in preparing this dish. So when someone says that my version takes them back to their childhood, it means that the essential flavours are on point.

Ingredients

1 whole bangus (milkfish)
    1½ to 2 pounds (750 grams to 1 kilogram)

banana leaf for steaming

Fish Skin Marinade

4 Tbsp (60 mL) soy sauce

4 Tbsp (60 mL) freshly squeezed lemon juice

sea salt to taste

pepper to taste

Batter

2 tsp (10 mL) whole black peppercorns

1 bunch cilantro, including roots and stems

10 cloves garlic

1 cup (250 mL) rice flour

2 tsp (10 mL) salt

½ tsp (2 mL) cayenne pepper

½ cup (125 mL) water

2 Tbsp (30 mL) fish sauce

Brunoise

4 Tbsp (60 mL) olive oil

5 cloves garlic, chopped finely

1 small onion, chopped finely

1 Roma tomato, diced

1 small potato, diced finely

1 small carrot, diced finely

½ cup (125 mL) frozen peas

¼ cup (60 mL) raisins

Tamarind Mixture

1 Tbsp (15 mL) tamarind paste

6 Tbsp (90 mL) tomato paste

1 tsp (5 mL) sugar

5 drops Worcestershire sauce

sea salt to taste

ground pepper to taste

½ cup panko-style bread crumbs plus more for coating

canola oil for frying (about 4 cups or 1 litre)

tomato rose for garnish (optional)

Preparation

(1) Scale fish and remove fins with scissors. Pound fish body with wooden mallet, and then massage. Make small slit with a paring knife on one side by the gills. Use an icing spatula or palette knife, separate fish meat from skin, taking care not to puncture skin.

(2) Squeeze fish meat out. Remove and discard viscera.

(3) Wrap fish meat in banana leaf, place in bamboo steamer, and cover with lid. Steam for approximately 5 minutes over pot filled with simmering water. Do not fully cook meat – just firm it up to make it easier to remove the bones.

(4) After the fish meat has cooled, get your sous-chef to remove the bones. Or do it yourself.

(5) Then turn fish skin inside out. Remove any remaining flesh and cut out any remaining bones.

(6) Now prepare marinade by placing soy sauce in marinating dish. Add lemon juice, sea salt, and pepper. Place fish skin into dish. Set aside.

(7) Prepare batter by placing peppercorns and a few drops of water in food processor. Grind coarsely. Peel garlic. For cilantro, lightly scrape the roots and chop the entire bunch, including roots and stems. Add garlic, chopped cilantro, rice flour, salt, and cayenne pepper to peppercorn mixture and blend to a smooth paste. Stir in water and fish sauce and whisk until well blended. Pour onto baking sheet, spread to edges, and refrigerate until needed.

(8) Prepare tamarind mixture by combining tamarind paste, tomato paste, sugar, and Worcestershire sauce in small bowl. Whisk to combine.

(9)   Finally, prepare brunoise by heating olive oil in sauté pan. Sauté garlic, onion, and tomato. Add finely diced potato and carrot. Stir-fry over medium heat until vegetables are tender. Add peas, raisins, and cooked fish meat. Add tamarind mixture. Season with salt and pepper. Cook about 5 minutes more. Remove from heat and let fish-meat mixture cool.

(10) When cool, add panko bread crumbs to fish-meat mixture, combining well. Stuff into fish skin through the slit by the gills. (Using a piping bag works well.)

(11) Heat canola oil in large pan.

(12) Coat stuffed fish in chilled batter. Dredge fish in panko-style breadcrumbs. Fry for approximately 3–5 minutes per side until golden brown. (Be careful when flipping; the head will want to fall off.) Remove from heat, blot on paper towel.

(13) To serve, arrange on platter with garnish as desired. For the play, scoop out small portions of stuffing and serve on small tasting plates with garnish as desired.

Equipment and Supplies

To prepare rellenong bangus during performance, the demonstration kitchen needs to be equipped with all necessary tools and utensils, including:

- bamboo steamer with lid and folded banana leaf
- wok
- several cutting boards
- chef's knife
- palette knife (or icing spatula)
- boning knife
- paring knife
- honing steel
- mallet
- kitchen shears
- sauté pan
- piping bag

Ingredients

- 1 milkfish
- other ingredients as listed in recipe
- prepared rellenong bangus (as emergency backup)

Sources

Below is the reading list that my director Guillermo Verdecchia supplied in the house program for the original 2010 production in Toronto. Some of these resources (like the books by Agoncillo and Constantino) were invaluable in providing background information for the show. Some make for excellent complementary reading for those who are interested in the ideas we've unpacked. And some are there for cheap laughs[33] (good luck finding those ones on Amazon).

Books

Agoncillo, Teodoro, and Oscar M. Guerroro. *The History of the Filipino People*. First published in mimeograph, 1960; now in its eighth edition, Quezon City: Malaya Books, 1990.

Constantino, Renato. *A History of the Philippines: From the Spanish Colonization to the Second World War*. New York: Monthly Review Press, 2010.

Cortés, Maximo. *I, Maximo: My Life, My Loves, My Food*, Volumes 1–7.

———. *Maximo's Maxims: Philosophy and Wisdom from the King of Chefs*.

---

33   The truth is that most of the funny lines in this play came from the incredible quick wit of Guillermo Verdecchia. It was a great process: I'd say something, he'd say something funny in response, I'd write down what he said and take credit for it. I should probably give him a percentage of my author's royalties. But I'm not going to.

————. *Me Cago en la Cocina Frances: El Manifesto Maximo de la Cocina Imperial.*

Goodall, Jane, with Gary McAvoy and Gail Hudson. *Harvest for Hope: A Guide to Mindful Eating.* New York: Warner Wellness / Hachette, 2005.

Issenberg, Sasha. *The Sushi Economy: Globalization and the Making of a Modern Delicacy.* New York: Gotham, 2007.

Kiple, Kenneth F. *A Movable Feast: Ten Millennia of Food Globalization.* Cambridge University Press, 2013.

Levenstein, Harvey A. *Paradox of Plenty: A Social History of Eating in Modern America.* Berkeley, CA: University of California Press, 1993; revised, 2003.

Nestle, Marion. *Food Politics: How the Food Industry Influences Nutrition and Health.* Berkeley, CA: University of California Press, 2002; revised and expanded, 2007; tenth anniversary edition with a foreword by Michael Pollan, 2013.

Patel, Raj. *Stuffed and Starved: The Hidden Battle for the World Food System.* Brooklyn, NY: Melville House, 2007.

Pollan, Michael. *In Defense of Food: An Eater's Manifesto.* New York: Penguin, 2008.

————. *The Omnivore's Dilemma: A Natural History of Four Meals.* New York: Penguin, 2006.

Schlosser, Eric. *Fast Food Nation: The Dark Side of the All-American Meal.* New York: Houghton Mifflin, 2001.

Sta. Maria, Felice Prudente. *The Governor-General's Kitchen: Philippine Culinary Vignettes and Period Recipes, 1521–1935.* Manila: Anvil Publishing, 2006.

Visser, Margaret. *Much Depends on Dinner: The Extraordinary History and Mythology, Allure and Obsessions, Perils and Taboos of an Ordinary Meal*. Toronto: McClelland and Stewart, 1986.

Weber, Karl, ed. *Food, Inc.: A Participant Guide: How Industrial Food Is Making Us Sicker, Fatter, and Poorer – And What You Can Do About It*. New York: Public Affairs, 2009.

Winne, Mark. *Closing the Food Gap: Resetting the Table in the Land of Plenty*. Boston: Beacon Press, 2008.

Articles

Appadurai, Arjun. "How to Make a National Cuisine." *Comparative Studies in Society and History* 30, no. 8 (January 1988): 3–24.

Harding, Jeremy. "What We're about to Receive." *London Review of Books* 32, no. 9 (May 13, 2010): 3–8.

Helstosky, Carol. "Recipe for the Nation: Reading Italian History through *La scienza in cucina* and *La cucina futurista*." *Food and Foodways* 11, no. 2–3 (2003): 113–40.

hooks, bell. "Eating the Other: Desire and Resistance." In *Black Looks: Race and Representation*, 21–39. Boston: South End Press, 1992.

Kirshenblatt-Gimblett, Barbara, and Doreen G. Fernandez "Culture Ingested: On the Indigenization of Philippine Food." *Gastronomica* 3, no. 1 (Winter 2003): 58–71:

———. "Making Sense of Food in Performance: The Table and the Stage." In *The Senses in Performance*, edited by Sally Banes and André Lepecki. 71–90. New York: Routledge, 2007.

Neuhaus, Jessamyn. "The Way to a Man's Heart: Gender Role, Domestic Ideology, and Cookbooks in the 1950s." *Journal of Social History* 32, no. 3 (1999): 529–55.

O'Connor, Kaori. "The King's Christmas Pudding: Globalization, Recipes, and the Commodities of Empire." *Journal of Global History* 4, no. 1 (March 2009): 127–55.

Philips, Lynn. "Food and Globalization." *Annual Review of Anthropology* 35 (2006): 37–57.

Super, John C. "Food and History." *Journal of Social History* 36, no. 1 (2002): 165–78.

Websites

Citizens for Public Justice. In particular, see Jennifer Heggland's article, "Come, Work, Leave: Temporary Foreign Workers in Canada," posted March 10, 2008. https://cpj.ca

Harvesting Freedom. A site advocating justice for migrant workers. harvestingfreedom.org

Migrant Workers in Canada. A blog about migrants in agriculture in Canada. migrantscanada.wordpress.com

United Food and Commercial Workers Union Canada. Recommendations published annually in a report on the status of migrant farm workers in Canada. www.ufcw.ca

CD

Dúos para los niños: Bono and Maximo Cortés Live at Wembley Stadium. Sony Records.

Acknowledgments

The original 2010 production of A Taste of Empire would not have been possible without the generous support of:

Byron Abalos, Martha Arima, Joanna Barrotta, Tara Beagan, Naomi Campbell, Donald Chan, Marjorie Chan, Jerry Doiron, Colin Doyle, Charlotte Empey, Joanna Falck, Kendra Fry, Deborah Hay, Esther Jun, Ulla Laidlaw, Richard Lee, Sandra Lefrançois, Peter Liepa, Joanne Lusted, Jackie Maxwell, Andy McKim, Chris Moffett, Dilani Mohan, Yvette Nolan, Darren O'Donnell, Alma Parry, Renna Reddie, Jenna Rodgers, Neha Ross, John Schrag, Christina Starr, Desirée Sy, Jonathan Sy, Lois Turk, Peter Turk, Nadine Villasin, David Yee, Dale Yim, and Jenny Young.

Also, Cahoots Theatre Company, Carlos Bulosan Theatre, Children's Peace Theatre, fu-GEN Theatre Company, Harbourfront Centre, Humber College, Mammalian Diving Reflex, Native Earth Performing Arts, Nella Cucina, Runnymede United Church, Shaw Festival, St. Lawrence Market, Theatre Passe Muraille, Canada Council for the Arts, and Ontario Arts Council.

A Taste of Empire got a second life on the West Coast in 2014 thanks to the wonderful souls at Boca del Lupo: Sherry Yoon, Jay Dodge, and Carey Dodge. Thanks also to Dani Fecko, Ming Hudson, Camyar Chaichian, Andrew Riseman, Natalie Gan, and Pedro Chamale.

Working on Derek Chan's translation in 2016, 食盡天下, was a joyous experience. For that, thanks to Rice & Beans Theatre (Derek Chan and Pedro Chamale), Teresa Leung, Curtis Li, Playwrights Theatre Centre, Playwrights' Workshop Montreal, Gateway Theatre, Briony Glassco, Emma Tibaldo, Molly Maguire, Bobby Theodore, and the Glassco Translation Residency in Tadoussac.

Thank you to Ann-Marie Metten, Chloë Filson, Callie Hitchcock, Leslie Smith, Vicki Williams, and Kevin Williams at Talonbooks.

Finally, special thanks to Nina Lee Aquino for providing the first opportunity to tell this story, to Ric Knowles for shepherding me through the final draft, to Guillermo Verdecchia for his Job-like patience in development, and to Leanna Brodie for always having faith.